Warning: Immigration Can Seriously Damage Your Wealth

Anthony Scholefield

© The Social Affairs Unit 2007
All Rights Reserved

British Library Cataloguing in Publication Data
A catalogue record of this book in available from the British Library

All views in this publication are those of the author, not those of the Social Affairs Unit,
its Trustees, Advisers or Director

Printed and bound in the United Kingdom by
imprintdigital.net

ISBN 978-1-904863-25-0

Social Affairs Unit
314-322 Regent Street
London W1B 5SA

www.socialaffairsunit.org.uk

Preface

When an immigrant steps off an aeroplane in London or New York, he arrives in a country whose native inhabitants have accumulated capital and wealth over generations and centuries. From the moment of arrival, he makes use of this wealth – the airports, the roads, the water supplies. Later, he requires the 'tools of production', housing, health services, churches, colleges and cultural institutions, etc.

British and American politicians and commentators have typically addressed the income or GDP effects of immigration; and, in the case of Britain, all major political parties regard these as favourable. They fail to mention that free market economists contend that immigration has a depressing effect on native wages.

The issue of the impact of immigration on *existing wealth* is rarely mentioned, though. The essence of this is as follows – when an immigrant worker arrives without capital and earns the same as a native worker, that means the wealth of the country is being shared among more people, and therefore wealth and capital per head are reduced.

To put it another way, how can an immigrant worker finance his initial stake in society – the same amount of wealth that the native workers have been building up over centuries?

This study draws two conclusions:

1. Capital is supplied for immigrants by depressing the wages of native workers. (This is an issue that the elite ignores – or about which it is 'in denial'.)

2. Even though native wages are depressed, this process will not fully supply an immigrant worker with his requisite share of wealth.

Natives lose out both ways:

- Their wages are reduced.
- Their wealth per head is reduced.

The process of depressing the wages of native workers also raises the question – is it socially and morally right to depress the earnings of native workers in order to provide capital and wealth for immigrants?

***

3

I would like to thank Michael Mosbacher of the Social Affairs Unit for his invitation to write this study and for his support during the writing. I would also thank Clive Liddiard for his excellent editing and help in clarifying both thought and language, as well as Gerald Frost, editor of *Eurofacts*, for allowing me to put forward some initial conclusions in articles for the magazine. Needless to say, they are not responsible for my conclusions, let alone any errors or inaccuracies.

The Author

Anthony Scholefield graduated from Christchurch, Oxford, in History. Later he took a degree in Economics and Statistics at London University and became a Chartered Accountant. After 25 years running a business in Central London, he became a founder of the UK Independence Party and its Secretary for three years. He has also written a study on demographic decline, *The Death of Europe*, and on the euro, *Why Britain Will not Join the Single Currency*.

Summary

British and American workers believe that immigration reduces their wages and their wealth. Conversely, the political elite of both countries, who benefit from cheaper labour, are in favour of having immigrant workers.

An analysis of the economic effects of immigration suggests that the impact on the wealth of natives is more important than the small effects of migration on the total GDP of natives, although there is a substantial impact on the distribution of income among natives.

Not for nothing did Adam Smith entitle his famous work, *An Inquiry into the Nature and Causes of the Wealth of Nations* and Karl Marx call his work, *Capital.* The effects of capital and wealth matter.

Indeed, the full economic impact of certain social and political factors that have come to the fore – such as longevity, fertility, migration, pensions and environmental issues – is to be grasped not merely through the short-term effect these factors have on GDP, but also through their effects on capital and wealth, which may be more marked and more important.

The fundamental economic benchmark relating to the economic effects of immigration is that put forward by the National Research Council of the USA, which states that 'if immigrants have exactly the same skill distribution as domestic workers and if they have brought sufficient capital with them to maintain the US capital/labor ratio, then natives will neither benefit nor lose from immigration'.

From this, our further analysis (using 2004 figures) concludes that *only* immigrant workers who bring £141,000 of capital per head into the UK (i.e. the amount of total British wealth divided by the total number of British workers), or £282,000 for a family of four; who make no foreign remittances; and who have at least the mean average skills of natives can possibly be of economic benefit to native Britons (this study excludes fiscal and national identity costs).

The average migrant worker contributes only £2,235 to the annual increase in the wealth of the country (£988 after foreign remittances).

Immigrant workers without £141,000 of capital must have that amount of capital instantly provided for them, or else they crowd in and appropriate part of the wealth of natives.

The argument as to the effect of immigration on native wages is binary: either the wages of natives fall after the arrival of immigrant workers or they do not.

Free market economists, such as those at the National Research Council of the USA and Professor Borjas in the USA, believe that the wages of workers competing with immigrants do fall, and indeed this is the basic law of supply and demand; but they also appear to believe, without much analysis however, that the process of capital adjustment means that the capital–labour ratio is subsequently restored, and that wage rates return to pre-immigration levels. This study shows that these arguments are incomplete, and that the capital adjustment process will not provide more than a fraction of the £282,000 of wealth required by each immigrant family.

The process of capital adjustment is quite clearly spelt out by economists, if not by politicians – falls in the wages of native workers fund the capital requirements of immigrants.

The alternative argument – that wages do not fall, and that the effect of increased supply has no effect on price – is put by the British government. This runs counter to the analysis of the American experts. Should government ministers and other pro-immigration supporters be correct, and wages do not fall, then there can be no capital adjustment and, therefore, every immigrant family's share of wealth of £282,000 must be appropriated from native workers.

Introduction

While many workers in rich countries such as the USA and Britain resent immigration, believing that it reduces their wages, worsens their conditions and makes inroads into their wealth, a large section of the elite and the political classes are in favour of it.

Both major political parties in Britain justify immigration and make enthusiastic remarks about it. For example, the Conservative manifesto of 2005 stated bluntly: 'Britain has benefited from immigration. We all gain from the social diversity, economic vibrancy and cultural richness that immigration brings.' Labour's 2005 manifesto said: 'Immigration has been good for Britain. Our philosophy is simple: if you are ready to work hard and there is work for you to do, you are welcome here.' The two major parties are, therefore, agreed that immigration is beneficial to native Britons – although, as in other policy areas, no cost benefit analysis has been done, so no effective debate can take place, as there is nothing substantive to debate at Westminster.

There are those who say that immigration does not and *must* not depress British wages. These include government ministers, the bishops of the Catholic Church and the Church of England, and the trade unions. The extraordinary effects of such thinking are indicated at the end of this paper: if such a situation existed, the main effect would be that immigrants could not possibly provide their own share of wealth and capital, and it would have to be appropriated from British natives.

It should be noted that wages earned by the latest wave of immigrants to the UK are extraordinarily low. Migration Watch reported (Economic Briefing Paper 1.12) that the Home Office's Accession Monitoring Report of August 2006 on the A8 EU Accession countries indicated 78 per cent of registered workers earned between £4.50 and £5.99 per hour. A further 15 per cent earned less than £8.00 per hour. As Migration Watch pointed out:

> This gives average annual earnings of £11,800. By comparison the average earnings of the employed working population overall was £22,000 in 2005. Thus earnings of A8 migrant workers was just over half those of the UK employed population as a whole.[1]

These figures are confirmed in a draft report for the Catholic bishops that is sympathetic to immigration. *The Ground of Justice*, prepared by the Von Hügel Institute of Cambridge University in 2007, surveyed a broad sample of Catholic immigrants, about 50 per cent of whom were from Eastern Europe:

> Overall, 50% of the surveyed immigrants earn £5.90 an hour or less. Only 25% earn more than £8 per hour and even the range above this is very limited in nature.[2]

Serious economic analysis, especially in the USA, assumes that any labour in competition with immigration will face depressed wages, but it argues that this will create higher profits for capital, which will lead to increased investment and restoration of the capital–labour ratio to pre-immigration levels. It should be noted that the main US studies, along with this study, agree that this process cannot improve the capital–labour ratio to above the pre-immigration level. While it seems to be a reasonable argument over the long term when considering output, a study of the statistics shows it to be unlikely when considering wealth.

In the USA, a survey conducted by the Chicago Council on Foreign Relations on differences of view between elites and voters showed (2002) that 60 per cent of the public viewed the present level of immigration as 'a critical threat to the vital interests of the United States', while only 14 per cent of the elite agreed with this – far and away the greatest divergence of view between elite and public opinion on any issue.[3] Then, in October 2006, a poll by the Polling Company revealed that only 3 per cent of the public supported increased levels of immigration, as contained in a proposal that was passed by a majority of the US Senate in 2006 and supported by President Bush.

As the American pollster, Scott Rasmussen, commented apropos the first of these polls: 'My own personal bias is, whenever I see a gap between the elites and the public, I tend to think the elites have something to learn, that they're missing some element of commonsense or not understanding the issue properly.'[4]

It is argued here that the public are indeed more attuned to the real economic costs of immigration, and that, on the part of the elites, there *is* a fundamental misunderstanding of the economic issues of migration.

There is also a raw divergence of interest here. As the owners of businesses, the business section of the elites gains from employing cheap labour, and all sections of the elite like cheap services in their private lives. At the same time, they are protected against competition from immigrants, because their own jobs place 'the greatest premium on mastery of the English language and culture'. This latter quotation, by Roy Beck of Numbers USA, a non-profit organization specializing in the study of population growth and the environment, also perfectly describes the situation regarding academia, the media and the Westminster village.[5]

The USA and the UK differ in one important respect: the UK is a country of both immigration and emigration; emigration from the US is very low. For example, in 2000, a World Bank report by Frédéric Docquier of the University of Lille estimated that the number of British tertiary-educated citizens living outside their native country was 1,542,011, compared to 428,078 US tertiary-educated citizens. This is in spite of the fact that the USA has five times the population of the UK. The upshot is that the rate of demographic change, based on changes occurring within the previous year, and taking into account both the number of those natives leaving a country and the number of non-natives coming in, is now much greater in the UK (0.66 per cent of the population in 2005) than in the USA (0.39 per cent).[6]

The large rise in immigration since 1997 has, then, been supported by business leaders such as Sir Digby Jones, former Director General of the CBI, who opined that 'an increase of one per cent in our population by immigration adds 1.5 per cent to our gross domestic product',[7] a statement that is patently absurd, as well as irrelevant to the incomes and wealth of British natives. (Incidentally, it is a fact that many journalists on conservative newspapers combine enthusiasm for immigration with denigration of the abilities of some of their fellow citizens.)

There has also been enthusiasm for the benefits of immigration in the Labour Party, among the Liberal Democrats and in other left-wing parties and organizations (as well as the institutions of the EU), despite their current claims to be – and actual historical role as – defenders of working people. This recently reached new levels, when, on the subject of East European migrants, TUC General Secretary Brendan Barber stated in September 2006: 'We favour the free movement of labour and intend to say so loud and clear.'[8]

So, we have big business and the multiculturalists in favour of immigration, and the elites benefiting from cheap labour in business and in their personal lives.

Needless to say, the political parties, running scared of the 'racism' charge and 'celebrating' diversity, seize on any favourable reference to immigration and amplify it.

As Professor Borjas, the famous US writer on immigration, concludes in his discussion of the US situation:

> The dangers also arise because there are powerful interest groups that gain substantially from current immigration policy. And these groups seem unable – or are unwilling – to see the cost the immigration imposes on other segments of society, and have considerable financial incentives and resources to influence the course of debate and to ensure that the current policy remains in place.
>
> The adverse effects of the second Great Migration will not go away simply because some people do not wish to see them. They will continue to accumulate. In the short run, these interest groups will likely succeed in delaying the day of reckoning. In the long run, their impact is much more perilous.[9]

The effects of immigration on wages are, therefore, not likely to trouble the elite and the political classes, because they are insulated from them.

No British analysis of the distribution of the depressing effects of immigration on different categories of income earners or wealth holders has been attempted. It is, however, harder for the elites to insulate themselves from the impact of immigration on wealth. One can, therefore, forecast that there will be a response from the elites to crowding-in – from which they cannot insulate themselves. Areas that could trigger a change in sentiment would include public transport crowding, road congestion, water shortages, overcrowding in housing, the impact of new housing on the environment, and the appropriation by the state of higher taxes to fund more schools, hospitals, etc.

Even if the elites are not personally too affected, the impact on wealth is spread much more widely among voters than is the effect of wage depression, so this is likely to produce more reaction from politicians. Indeed, on 18 April 2007, the Home Office Immigration Minister, Liam Byrne, was quoted in the *Daily Mail* as saying that mass immigration had left the country 'deeply unsettled'. He called for 'a more open debate about what immigration is good for Britain that takes into account its wider impact'.

Free market economists

One other group is also in favour of immigration – the free market economists who believe in the analogy between free migration and free trade. This academic and intellectual backing for immigration is influential, especially with 'conservative' opinion formers. It is associated with such diverse bodies as the *Wall Street Journal*, which calls for open borders in the USA, and the Centre for the New Europe and Open Europe, both of which call for an open door to immigration into Britain from all EU countries.

It is their stance – incorrect, in the opinion of this study – that has hamstrung the emergence of a respectable questioning of the foundations of the pro-immigration economic arguments.

Nevertheless, the bulk of this study will deal with their analysis.

In the view of these free market economists, classic economic theory shows that if all factors of production (excluding land) are allowed to flow freely worldwide, this will produce the most output in the world. (This entails free trade and free movement of capital and labour.) According to this theory, migrants will flow across the world until the wages on offer in migrant-receiving countries are at the level of the wages on offer in the migrants' original home countries, plus the costs and disbenefits of migration.
Their analysis of the impact on production is perfectly correct – in a narrow sense. But this paper argues that it is an incomplete analysis and ignores much of the economic impact of immigration.

In the USA – unlike in Britain – a great deal of work has been done on the economics of immigration, and the free migration argument is put by the National Research Council (NRC) of the National Academy of Sciences in its much-quoted work, *The New Americans*, which was commissioned by the US Congress:

> The primary effect of both immigration and international trade is to allow us to specialize in producing those things we are good at and to consume something other than what we can produce ourselves.

> Exactly the same reasons that explain the net national gain from trading with other countries explain the net national gain from immigration. First, a gain arises from shifting productive resources towards more valuable activities. Another gain flows from shifting consumption towards commodities whose cost has fallen. Although some people in the trading countries may be harmed by this specialization, the important lesson, as we have seen, is that the gains from trade outweigh the losses.[10]

And, further:

> Broadly speaking, immigration and international trade are alternative ways to achieve the same goal. Through either mechanism, we can obtain inputs that are relatively more abundant overseas than they are in our own country. Given the high level of human capital (skill) in the United States, we can import low-skilled workers (through immigration) or we can import the goods such workers make.[11]

The NRC did introduce the caveat that this analysis referred to a static situation, a moment-in-time analysis.

But, despite being correct in its narrow, static analysis of production, it is not a proper and full economic analysis of immigration, as it ignores the impact on wealth, with its major effects on the standard of living and overall economic well-being. In other words, the NRC work covers only part of the economic picture. It concentrates on income effects and ignores wealth effects.

It will be shown later that both the NRC and Professor Borjas avoid saying that immigration will provide increased wealth or higher per capita GDP for natives. They simply assume, with little or no analysis, that capital adjustment at the expense of native wage earners will restore the capital–labour ratio in GDP to its pre-immigration level.

Furthermore, it is apparent from close study that, when both the NRC and Professor Borjas refer to capital, they are referring to what Henry Hazlitt calls 'the tools of production', and not to the whole wealth of a country. Neither the NRC nor Professor Borjas discusses the effects of immigration on wealth, or how immigration can restore the wealth–labour balance to its pre-immigration level. This study makes an (admittedly rough) effort to do so and shows how unlikely it is to return to its previous level.

11

In *The New Americans*, the NRC studied the fiscal effects of immigration, and included there the impact of immigration on taxes and benefits. Some of these benefits, such as education, health and public service provision by government, included additions to wealth. The NRC assumed these additions to wealth would maintain the level of wealth that existed in these areas prior to the arrival of immigrants. The results showed that, in the two states on which the data were based, California and New Jersey, there was a great shortfall between the taxes paid by immigrants and the benefits received by them. The analysis did not provide a breakdown to disentangle capital additions from current spending and transfer payments, and it is far from certain that, when the basis for the analysis was set up, all the costs of capital spending to provide for immigrants were allocated solely to immigrants. Moreover, these estimates have a large number of assumptions built into them. Many of these assumptions have been questioned by experts such as Professor Borjas. It therefore seems simpler to approach the subject from a different angle: to establish the existing wealth of natives and then show that immigrants cannot generate the same wealth for themselves.

The gains and losses of migration ('the immigration surplus')

The NRC work also made a lengthy analysis of the impact of immigration on factors of production.

The NRC study is written in an elegant and balanced style, and, not surprisingly, is very often quoted in immigration studies in the USA.

It states that 'an increase in immigration flows will lead to higher income for productive factors that are complementary with immigrants, but lower incomes for factors that compete with immigrants'.[12]

It then demonstrates convincingly that the theoretical effect of an immigration that is without capital and that has skills different from those of the natives is to create a net increase in native GDP. It is most important to note that the NRC calculation of the 'immigration surplus' specifically assumes that the new labour requires no wealth! – no houses, schools, water supplies, etc.

This process is achieved by reducing the wages of natives and increasing returns to capitalists and complementary labour. As a side effect, there is an immigration surplus created by the arrival of immigrants who do not retain all the product they create – some of this product is diverted to capital or complementary labour. The technical argument for the gains and losses of immigration (or the 'immigration surplus') is contained in Appendix A.

But calculations by the NRC, Professor Borjas and others show that this immigration surplus, based on the then current immigration labour force in the USA, is very small ($1–10 billion per annum for the US economy in 1996, when the US GDP was $7,000 billion) and that there are substantial distribution effects away from native labour, which competes with immigrants, to capital and complementary labour.

However, the NRC emphasized that 'It is only because immigrants and native workers differ from each other that immigration yields a net national gain.'[13]

The NRC also examined the case where immigrants have the *same* skill distribution and capital as natives, and found no gain for natives in this scenario:

> If immigrants have exactly the same skill distribution as domestic workers…and if they have brought sufficient capital with them to maintain the US capital/labor ratio, then natives will neither benefit nor lose from immigration. In this case, all inputs and national output will increase by the same amount and the wages of all workers will remain constant.[14]

It is clear from this quotation, with its reference to output, that the NRC only considers capital as being the 'tools of production' and does not consider wealth.

On the face of it, the NRC conclusions appear astonishing and perverse. How can the economic well-being of American natives increase as a result of an influx of unskilled and capital-less workers, while it does not increase following an influx of workers with the same skills and capital as native Americans? In fact, the explanation for the apparently perverse outcome is that the NRC ignores the effects on wealth. (And, of course, for a full analysis it is necessary to consider the fiscal and cultural effects of migration, which are not treated here. The most likely economic benefit of migration – the one-off provision of nurtured and educated adults from another economy – falls within the fiscal sphere.) This paper will endeavour to address the contradictions.

The NRC also points out that:

> if the children of immigrants are just like the children of the native born, we are back to the case in which all we are doing is scaling up the population and economy with no impact on per capita incomes. A generation of increased immigration then can alter long-term growth paths only if generational assimilation, both economic and demographic, is never complete.[15]

This careful study, therefore, concludes that the immigration of those with the same skills and capital as natives does not benefit natives. It also concludes that, as immigrants come to be like the native born, all that happens is that we see an increase in population and GDP, with no effect on the per capita GDP of natives.

The only economic benefit of present immigration in the USA comes about if immigrants are different from native workers, cause a fall in some native wages and, as a by-product, produce $1–10 billion net GDP gain for natives overall, both to complementary labour and capital, reducing each year as the immigrants assimilate. The NRC analysis does not consider the effects of such immigration on wealth.

It is, of course, possible to envisage immigrants who have higher skills than the natives and who bring in more capital per head with them than the natives possess. In this case, the overall per capita GDP of the new, combined native/immigrant population will rise, compared to the pre-existing native per capita GDP. Such immigrations are typical of the settlement of the Europeans in the New World and Australasia, or of modern Israel.

So, the NRC's findings can be summarized thus:

- The current influx into the US of immigrants whose skills or capital are *different* from those of natives creates a very small net addition to the per capita GDP of natives (about 0.10 per cent). This analysis of the net gains of immigration ignores the required provision of wealth to immigrants.

- An influx of immigrants whose skills and capital are the *same* as those of natives does not increase the per capita GDP of natives.

- The immigration surplus is created because of the difference between the skills of natives and of immigrants. As these shrink, so the benefit to natives' per capita GDP shrinks and eventually disappears.

The logic of the above is that, once the difference between natives and migrants disappears, there is no further benefit to natives, and therefore there can be no long-term situation where the per capita GDP of natives is increased by immigration, unless the immigrants have more skills and capital than natives.

As the first and second finding appear contradictory and perverse, it is necessary to examine why both propositions are true. The explanatory link is to be found in an analysis of the effects of immigration on wealth and capital (see below).

Comparisons with the USA

Another argument to be considered is that of pro-immigration enthusiasts, who point to the USA and state that it is an economy based on immigration and has the highest standard of living in the world – therefore immigration must be beneficial to native Americans. In reality, US economic success is based on its productivity and relatively free economy. The difference between it and the rest of the world was greatest between 1924 and 1965 – during a period of low immigration. If immigration promotes a higher standard of living, then Argentina, which received proportionately even more immigrants than the USA in the late nineteenth century, would be richer than the countries from which the immigrants came, such as Italy, Germany and Spain. It is not. A journalist such as Luke Johnson can castigate Japan for its low immigration rate and state: 'This lack of fresh blood may be one reason why, until recently, their economy had significantly stagnated for over 12 years.'[16] Apparently, lack of fresh blood had not stopped the Japanese economy being highly successful until 1990. Mr Johnson fails to consider whether it might have been Japan's economic policies that caused this problem of stagnation in 1990, rather than the need for fresh blood that apparently mysteriously surfaced just then.

Much of the argument suggesting benefits of immigration into the USA is, on closer examination, based on the *total growth* of the US economy, rather than on *growth per head of population*:

> Thus, the size of the economy, measured, say, by real gross domestic product (GDP) grew more rapidly than it would have without immigration. This is, we think, what historian Maldwyn Allen Jones had in mind when he wrote in his classic book, *American Immigration*:
>
>> 'The realization of America's vast economic potential has...been due in significant measure to the efforts of immigrants. They supplied much of the labor and technical skill to tap the under-developed resources of a virgin continent...'
>
> But this concept of growth, sometimes called 'extensive growth', is not what economists usually mean by the phrase 'economic growth'. Instead the growth of labor productivity, or the growth of per capita output, or the growth in the standard of living – 'intensive growth' – is usually of greater interest... If per capita output is to grow, GDP must grow faster than the population. So the question becomes: Does immigration increase or reduce labor productivity?[17]

There is, in fact, some dispute as to whether, for example, the massive immigration into the US at the end of the nineteenth century did increase the per capita GDP of native Americans. Much of the supporting argument is based on the boost given to the increase in the ratio of the working population to the total population, because most immigrants were young workers; but this is obviously a one-off effect. For this argument to have permanent validity, there would have to be a never-ending immigration of new, young workers.

The second argument put forward is one of increased returns to scale, with large pools of capital and labour reducing costs. This argument seems a reasonable one, but is unproven. There is, of course, the opposite argument of the costs of congestion.

Neglect of wealth effects

To understand why those who advocate free movement of labour are wrong to view free movement of labour as analogous to free trade, it is essential to place discussion of the economics of migration on a proper and full basis, and to include a discussion of the effects on wealth.

It is also useful to clarify the position using some numbers – generally thin on the ground in pro-immigration arguments.

As Professor Borjas states:

> Instead, many observers simply discuss the potential sources of the economic benefits, do a lot of hand waving, and often insinuate that these benefits must be very large. On the rare occasions when actual numbers are provided, there is seldom any documentation to substantiate the often-exaggerated claims.[18]

At all times, this study considers a totally free market with no welfare state. It does not consider the fiscal effects of immigration, such as taxation and welfare. It assumes constant returns to scale, and it does not consider the externalities of immigration. It assumes that all existing investment is exactly correct for the native population. It assumes each worker has only one dependant.

The core argument is that any addition to the population, whether through increased fertility or immigration without capital, must require capital and wealth to be provided for the newcomers. Either this is supplied by the newcomers alone (in which case, assuming wages similar to those of natives, they can never catch up with natives, who have already accumulated wealth) or it is appropriated from natives, by a process the NRC calls 'assimilation', and apportioned to newcomers, in which case the natives suffer a loss of wealth. In one case, newcomers never catch up with natives and so cannot add to natives' wealth; in the other, the natives suffer an outright loss of wealth.

The only exception to this, as already mentioned, would be if newcomers were so skilled or so wealthy that they could provide for themselves the wealth the natives have accumulated over generations and centuries. Such newcomers to the USA and Britain do exist, but they are few in number. Only five out of 582,000 new arrivals in Britain in 2004 came under permits issued to persons 'of independent means'. As for the USA, in *The New Americans* the NRC quotes data from the US Immigration and Naturalization Service, showing that in 1995 10,465 visas were available for allocation to investors and their families, but only 540 were taken up – within an immigration total of 720,461. In effect, therefore, immigration should only be offered to those who bring with them capital of at least £282,000 for a family of four (according to the calculations below) and who have skills that are better than the average among natives, or who can accumulate the £282,000 of savings in a short time.

In any case, the argument in favour of the free movement of labour is not one of selecting a few, carefully picked, super-skilled or extremely wealthy immigrants: it is an argument for open doors.

There are three points to consider in distinguishing free migration from free trade.

First, as the NRC points out, there is a difference in concept. Immigration, in terms of permanent settlement immigration, is a transfer of stock, while trade is a flow: 'an immigrant who comes permanently to the United States competes with natives for every year of his or her working life. Trade is a flow, dependent on exchange rates and trade policies...'[19]

Furthermore, an influx of goods has no effect on the accumulated wealth of an economy, such as homes, water supply, schools, roads, etc. An influx of people has an enormous effect.

Second, while some economists quite correctly point out that total world output would increase if factors flowed freely, every government is, by its mandate, focused on maximizing economic gains for the native population. While it can be demonstrated that free trade would benefit a country (albeit with winners and losers within that country), free immigration would mean that nearly the entire distribution of the gains from free immigration would go either to the immigrants or to the inhabitants of the countries from which the immigrants came (apart from the small immigration surplus in production, which ignores the deleterious effects on the wealth of the natives).

After all, various calculations as to the effect on the USA of the arrival of 10 per cent of its workforce from abroad show the immigration surplus – that is, the value to native Americans – to have been in the range of $1–10 billion in 1996. Of course, the benefits to migrants are large, since they earn much greater incomes in the USA than they did in their home countries. The benefits to the native population are conversely tiny and are accompanied by serious distribution problems (as well, of course, as fiscal costs and national identity concerns). As Professor Borjas states, 'the net gain seems much too small to justify such a grand social experiment'.[20]

Third, and most important, is the effect of immigration on wealth, as well as on production.

Balance-sheet effects are usually neglected in economic theory, and much modern economic analysis concentrates on micro-economic income effects.

However, when considering the standard of living of natives, we must take account of the accumulated wealth of a country, and this is not reflected in GDP figures.

Not for nothing did Adam Smith entitle his famous work, *An Inquiry into the Nature and Causes of the Wealth of Nations* and Karl Marx call his work, *Capital.*

Income and wealth are, of course, closely interconnected, with more income increasing wealth, and wealth in turn helping to increase income.

Most economic discussion on migration has concentrated on the impact of migration on income or GDP; but this is only part of the picture.

To take a simple point, all that is reflected in GDP figures for housing is the annual addition, which in Britain is around 135,000 houses (net) per annum, plus the cost of repairs, etc. The existence of 20 million houses plays no part in GDP calculations, but does play an immense part in wealth and 'standard of living'. All other 'created assets', such as roads, schools, factories, etc., play the same role.

To consider the standard of living of a country's inhabitants, we must not only take account of the income and expenditure account, or GDP, but also the wealth or balance sheet. Standard of living does not depend solely on GDP: it also depends on the use of the accumulated wealth, such as houses, buildings, roads, factories, water supplies, power stations and a myriad other items. These are not reflected in GDP, except in the form of marginal annual additions.

The NRC analysis refers to this aspect in just one brief footnote to the passage quoted below:

> Similarly, if the children of immigrants born in the United States distribute themselves among the skilled and unskilled labor force and also save and invest in the same way as natives, the effects of an increase in immigration over one generation will be negligible one generation following that.[21]

The footnote reads:

> This abstracts from secondary effects, such as the physical capital required to transform immigrant children into skilled workers, which immigrants did not bring with them.[22]

In reality, the capital required is not simply that required to make skilled workers, but is also the social capital or wealth required to bring immigrants up to the standard of living of natives.

And the secondary effects are enormous.

Henry Hazlitt – the importance of capital

As the great American economic journalist, Henry Hazlitt, wrote:

> Almost the whole wealth of the modern world, nearly everything that distinguishes it from the preindustrial world of the seventeenth Century, consists of its accumulated capital.
>
> This capital is made up of many things that might better be called consumers' durable goods – automobiles, refrigerators, furniture, schools, colleges, churches, libraries, hospitals and, above all private homes...
>
> The second part of capital is what we may call capital proper. It consists of the tools of production...[23]

British wealth – how much is it?

Now seems a good time to flesh the argument out with some figures.

The wealth of the British people was estimated by National Statistics to total £4,245 billion in 2004[24] (this excludes consumer durables, except houses, and it also excludes land). Strictly speaking, it is the value of 'created assets' at replacement cost, at 2003 prices. It has been calculated that the national wealth in 1948 – for a considerably smaller population – was £1,005 billion, again using 2003 prices. It should probably be noted, as an example of the neglect of wealth issues, that the National Statistics tables on the value of 'created assets' state quite erroneously that these were calculated at 1995 prices. This makes quite a difference, but National Statistics has not noticed the error. Nevertheless, the increased wealth per head means that wealth effects become more and more important in any consideration of the effects of migration in the modern era.

The accumulation of capital is dependent on many sources: the intensity of the labour force, numbers, skills, time, efforts, technology, entrepreneurial skills, etc. What we have to do is isolate the impact of migratory labour on capital accumulation.

Total fixed capital formation in 2004 was £190 billion, and capital consumption was £123 billion. This meant a net addition to capital stock of £67 billion, or 1.58 per cent of wealth. In other words, the wealth of the UK amounts to roughly sixty years' worth of capital additions.

Some of this wealth – for example, machinery – depreciates quickly, but other capital stock has been accumulated over centuries, such as Oxbridge colleges, railways, dams, sewage works, etc. In the case of dwellings, there were 20.9 million in 2003, including a net addition of 134,000, or an addition to the capital stock of 0.64 per cent, which means the capital stock is about 150 years' production. The *Independent* newspaper once calculated – and it seems a realistic estimate – that 95 per cent of British roads were laid down before 1900, and, of course, the same applies to railways.

With 30 million workers in Britain, one can say that the total wealth per worker is £4,245 billion divided by 30 million, which is £141,000 per worker. In the following calculations, each worker is assumed to have one dependant.

Each worker contributes £2,235 per annum (£67 billion divided by 30 million) to improve the country's capital, taking his share of capital additions either direct or via enterprises he works in.

Obviously, higher earners contribute more, as most lower wage earners save little; but £2,235 is the average.

The impact of immigration

The arrival of a migrant worker means that he instantly requires £141,000 of capital in order to bring his stock of wealth into line with that of natives, yet he contributes (assuming he is an average worker) only £2,235 per annum to capital formation. If the newcomer does not instantly supply the £141,000 capital, there is wealth dilution for natives. (Note that, for a family of four, including two workers, this actually means a requirement of £282,000, as all the calculations are done on the basis of the current labour force distribution of one worker to one dependant.)

A further point is that overseas remittances from Britain totalled £3.8 billion in 2003. If the foreign born constitute 10 per cent of the workforce, as estimated by the Home Office, they should contribute 10 per cent of £67 billion to capital formation, which is £6.7 billion; however, if the £3.8 billion of remittances is attributed solely to the foreign born, then their contribution to capital formation is only 44 per cent of the £2,235 required, or £988 per worker.

One can consider the matter like this. A native worker has a capital bank account of £141,000, and adds £2,235 to it each year. A migrant worker has a capital bank account of nil and adds £988 per annum. It takes the immigrant 150 years (ignoring interest effects) to accumulate the capital the native has at the outset. In those 150 years, the native adds a further £336,000 to his capital bank account, making a total of £477,000.

The Economic Institute of the Dutch government has done some useful work on the effects on GDP when an immigrant arrives without capital.[25]

With a fixed capital stock and an immigration workforce of 5 per cent of the whole, total GDP is increased by 2.4 per cent if all immigrants are unskilled; 2.9 per cent if the skill mix of immigrants is the same as that of natives; and 3.2 per cent if all immigrants are highly skilled. In all cases, the average per capita GDP of natives and immigrants combined falls below the per capita GDP of natives *before immigration*, because there is less capital per worker. In all cases, the wages of skilled and non-skilled workers fall and the return to capital increases. And, of course, the wealth of natives is reduced, because more people are trying to use the same amount of wealth.

Of course, a small number of high-earning migrants will pay for their requisite stock of wealth of £141,000 immediately or over a very short period; but the average immigrant, who, according to Home Office estimates, earns the same as natives, contributes only £988 per head per annum to the £141,000 required to bring him up to the native's wealth. Moreover, the native worker is already backed by £141,000 and is adding £2,235 per annum, so the wealth gap is widening.

This study concludes, therefore, that only those immigrant workers who a) bring in £141,000 of capital per worker with them, b) make no foreign remittances, and c) have at least the mean average skills of natives do not dilute the wealth of natives. This runs counter to the statements both of the Labour Party and of the Conservative Party.

A word of warning here for those who advocate the immigration of skilled workers.[*] We have already seen that natives cannot benefit from the immigration of workers who have a skill and capital profile that is identical to that of natives. The arrival of workers who have higher skills but little or no capital can only be beneficial if their skills are so high that they can generate the requisite capital within a short time. We can see that the requisite capital is estimated to be at least £282,000 for a family of four, when the average capital generated per worker is £2,235 per annum. The benefit of skilled immigrants, therefore, depends on whether the £282,000 can be quickly generated, and (ignoring foreign remittances) this depends on the level of capital generated being several multiples of the £2,235 capital generated by the average worker. In other words, for skilled workers to be beneficial, they would have to be very high earners indeed – and high personal savers – certainly in the top 20 per cent of the workforce. The interest implications of providing £282,000 of instant capital for two immigrant workers plus two dependants means that the payback

---

[*] 'Skilled' is defined here as 'having skills better than the mean level of skill of natives'. Earnings are an approximation of skill, and mean average earnings are considerably higher than median average wages.

period must be short, or else the £282,000 will be freighted with high interest costs.

An interesting illustration of the importance of wealth effects (and one that demonstrates that GDP is not the only measurement to be taken into account) is supplied by the arrival of British retirees on the Spanish Costas. They, of course, do not work and do not contribute to GDP as workers. It is assumed that each individual has one dependant. For them to be of economic benefit to Spain, they would have to bring with them an income stream that produces sufficient taxes to take care of the fiscal costs to Spain, plus, of course, an adequate income to live on. They also have a wealth effect, as they use Spanish roads, hospitals, houses, public buildings, etc. Assuming the same wealth backing as the average Briton, they would need to invest £141,000 per head in Spain, plus a further £2,235 per annum in addition to their financial contributions. This £141,000 could be in loan form, assuming there were no descendants living in Spain.

Temporary migration

The arrival of temporary migrants without capital is little different from having permanent migrants arrive. Temporary migration to take part in the general economy needs to be distinguished from specialized activity, such as a one-off construction project – for example, an oilfield in a Middle Eastern desert – for which migrant labour is recruited on a temporary basis and for which the 'created assets' are supplied by the employer as part of the project costs and are depreciated over the lifetime of the project. Temporary immigrants into the general economy also require wealth in the form of housing, 'tools of production', water supplies, roads, power, etc. There may, of course, be marginal differences, such as a lower call on educational resources if they do not have children with them, and they may occupy more crowded and inferior housing. Whether or not the latter is beneficial is a value judgement. Government ministers, the bishops of the Catholic Church and the Church of England and the media would state that it is not tolerable. They also may not have the language skills of the host community – and this generates an extra burden.

All in all, a temporary migrant worker will require only a marginally smaller share of wealth to be allocated to him than a permanent migrant, and, of course, there is less chance of him paying for his wealth needs through economic contributions, since, by definition, these are short term.

If we take the arguments of the free market economists in favour of migration, and apply them to temporary migration and its effects on wealth, we can see that the arrival of temporary migrants causes a fall in the wages of competing native labour and a shift of income to complementary labour and capital. It is then

22

claimed that the capital–labour ratio is restored by capital adjustment. Obviously, if migration is temporary, this process ceases and goes into reverse on the departure of the temporary migrants. Labour that is competing with the temporary migrant gains, while complementary labour and capital lose. The process of capital adjustment is thrown into reverse. It is thus an expensive and costly waste of money. To take just one example: a farmer who expands his crops and supporting capital equipment on the basis of a supply of only temporary labour will misallocate and waste his investment when the temporary labour is withdrawn.

Temporary migration actually leads to a misallocation and waste of capital.

Migrants without capital

What happens when the immigrant worker does not have £141,000 of capital with him? We then have the phenomenon of 'crowding-in'. Immigrants use dwellings more intensively; they overload transport, water resources and all the other accumulated capital (we assume the native economy is in equilibrium). Production per head decreases, because there is capital dilution and so each worker has fewer 'tools of production'. As the *National Institute Economic Review* (No. 198, October 2006) pointed out: 'For each extra pair of hands income rises less in proportion because there is no extra capital.' This diverts some capital from the job of intensifying the wealth of natives to that of supplying the needs of immigrants – either voluntarily, by the means of capital readjustment described below, or through government taxation. So, the increase in the capital backing of the natives is reduced, and there may also be some diversion of natives' consumption into supplying capital to immigrants. Immigration, therefore, reduces the wealth and consumption of natives.

Thus, not only is the per capita GDP of the new, combined workforce of natives and immigrants reduced below the previous per capita GDP of natives by the effects of immigration without capital, as the Dutch Economic Institute study shows, but so is the accumulation of the wealth of natives, their standard of living, and also, therefore, their future production.

The NRC and Professor Borjas use such words as 'assimilation' and 'capital adjustment' to describe the merging of immigrants into the economy. In fact, the process is one of appropriation of capital from natives, either by means of taxation or through diversion of capital. While the appropriation of capital for immigrants in housing, education, etc. may be visible in extra taxation and council taxes, diversion of capital is less obvious, though it is no less powerful.

An indication of how the wealth of UK natives will be appropriated is shown by the sort of comments 'respected' commentators make in *The Londoner*, the house magazine of Ken Livingstone, indicating the scale of appropriation required to produce the necessary capital and wealth for immigrants.

According to Ian Barlow, a senior partner with KPMG:

> The amount of people using public transport in London is set to grow by more than a third in the next few years… Money must come forward [*sic*] for things like Crossrail. London also needs cheaper housing and more skills' training.

Tony Travers, the director of the Greater London Group of the London School of Economics, added:

> If London is to grow the way the government says it wants to, then [ministers must invest] in the capital's infrastructure. Transport, schools, hospitals, roads and everything else that makes a city work will all have to have more money spent on them.

The diversion of capital investment occurs as capitalists re-rank the profitability of investments after immigration. Where increased returns are available because of immigration, some investment will be made in these areas and, therefore, some investment will not be made in the lower-return areas that increase native wealth or production. Of course, one reason why there are lower returns in some areas is that native wages have been depressed by immigration, so native workers who are in competition with migrants suffer not only from lower wages but also from diversion of capital.

As indicated above, this phenomenon is similar (though more accentuated) to that engendered by an increase in the native population of workers through increased fertility. It also suggests why the employment of non-workers in the native population (the unemployed, women workers, the retired) is so beneficial, as their employment is a pure gain, since, as dependants of the workers, they are already users of capital. The transfer of a person from being a dependant to a worker means there is an extra contributor to capital formation each year but no extra requirement for wealth use, except for the tools of production.

The theory of capital adjustment

Up to now, the analysis has been largely static, with capital and wealth regarded as fixed. It is necessary now to look at the dynamic effects on capital and wealth.

This is contained within the theory of capital adjustment following an influx of immigrants, since this is the core argument of pro-immigration economists that immigration benefits natives – or at any rate does not harm them. Though John Meadowcroft of the Institute of Economic Affairs has stated that immigration will make a country richer on account of making available 'freed capital to be put to more productive use elsewhere', it is important to note that this is not a claim made by the American immigration experts.[26]

Any arguments that migration benefits native workers centre on the increased returns to capital, which create a fresh demand for workers and a new equilibrium, with higher levels of capital and employment (but not higher amounts of capital per head).

It should be noted that the leading American academics, such as the NRC and Professor Borjas, do not claim that the increased returns to capital will do any more than restore native wages to the pre-immigration level. In its second major study, entitled *The Immigration Debate*, the NRC stated: 'We are not, of course, suggesting that immigration caused an improvement in real wages.'[27] This fits in logically with the NRC analysis quoted earlier, demonstrating that, once immigrants acquire skills and capital similar to those of the natives, the economy will simply enlarge pro rata. So the American academics (and, incidentally, the Dutch Economic Institute) believe that increased returns to capital are only effective up to the point at which immigrants have the same skills and capital as natives.

This must be the logical conclusion.

Furthermore, the NRC states:

> As already mentioned, in the short run the influx of new labor is likely to depress the capital–labor ratio before it is restored through new investment. If the capital stock is disproportionately owned by native-born residents…then native-born owners of capital will benefit temporarily from higher returns to capital. Indeed, it is this higher return to capital that (in part) is thought to induce an increased volume of investment that ultimately restores the capital–labor ratio to its pre-immigration level.[28]

The theory of capital adjustment makes it clear that money taken away from native workers is used to fund the capital required by immigrants. Capitalists are an intermediary in this process.

The argument (and, once again, it must be emphasized that this is *not* suggested by the NRC or by Professor Borjas) that immigration benefits natives through the mechanism of capital adjustment has formidable hurdles to surmount. To start with, nearly all economic theorists – as the Dutch Economic Institute states and the NRC concludes – believe migration in the short run, with capital fixed, reduces the earnings of natives and increases the return to capital.

In its study, the NRC outlines the mechanism by which migration restores the capital–labour ratio: by initially depressing natives' wages, increasing returns to capital, drawing in more capital, and thus establishing a new equilibrium. In other words, for native labour earnings to stabilize, they must first fall. This seems a wayward path. Nor is there much academic support for it. As the NRC reports: 'The second key point – the impact of immigration on capital formation – has been left largely to assumption and speculation.'[29]

In any event, the capital adjustment process centres on restoring the amount of tools of production, not on total wealth.

To say that immigration benefits natives in Britain today, the following logical hurdles must be cleared:

1) The immigrant must accumulate the same amount as the average wealth held by native workers. This figure, in 2004 in Britain, was estimated to be £141,000 per worker. Because we assume one dependant per worker, which is the present state of the British labour force, a family of four would require £282,000 of capital.

2) The immigrant must then pay interest on the wealth appropriated from natives (or elsewhere) to support him for as long as it takes him to accumulate the requisite £141,000.

3) He must then also match the further capital additions generated by native workers during the period when the immigrant is generating his stake capital of £141,000 (plus interest). (The native worker adds £2,235 per annum.)

4) Only *then* does the immigrant reach a point of equality of contribution with natives. For him actually to benefit natives, he must generate a *further* increase in capital, *beyond* the native's yearly increase in capital that he must match.

There are two sources (excluding non-measurable costs and benefits) of an immigrant's contribution to wealth accumulation:

- savings by the worker out of his own wages directly or in the form of profits to the enterprise in which he is employed; and
- savings by capitalists out of the extra returns to capital, due to a fall in the wages paid to native labour.

In actual fact, depending on what activities the government is engaged in, some of the process of capital addition is in the hands of government. Some government activities are core areas, such as roads, order and justice; other areas, such as health, education, railways, may fall partly or generally within the government area. The government appropriates part of workers' wages and

26

enterprise profits to carry out its activities, some of which entail capital additions to wealth.

By definition, the first of the sources of contribution (for the average worker) can only be item (3) above, less overseas remittances. So the whole burden of generating the remainder of the wealth required in items (1), (2) and (4) falls on the added return to the extra savings of capitalists, which, of course, are also reduced by the lesser savings now being made by native workers out of their reduced wages. (Workers are also capitalists in relation to their own savings, pension funds, etc.)

Professor Borjas also notes:

> as the capital stock inevitably adjusts to the changed economic environment, the immigration surplus will tend to become smaller and smaller and, in the end natives may be neither better off nor worse off because of immigration.[30]

So, for natives, the whole process of immigration means initial losses, immense dislocation, reduced production per head, a reduction in the standard of living due to wealth dilution, with the ultimate result that the capital–labour ratio is restored to its pre-immigration level – or, put another way, 'as you were'. This is not a good deal for natives, since we show below that the calculations of capital adjustment do not return wealth to its pre-immigration level.

There is simply no respectable argument that immigration will ever generate added returns for natives, unless immigrants have skills and capital that are superior to those of natives. At best, as the NRC shows very logically in its analysis, once the immigrants acquire skills and capital similar to those possessed by natives, GDP will simply enlarge pro rata.

Calculations of capital adjustment – are they realistic?

Professor Borjas calculates that the 10 per cent of the US workforce that is immigrant would, in his central projection, generate an increase of 3 per cent in the total income of capitalists in the USA at the expense of labour. Conveniently for calculation, this is approximately 1 per cent of US GDP (capital takes about one third of US GDP).

If one transposes this extremely rough calculation to the UK, which also has an immigration labour force that totals 10 per cent of the whole and a similar split in returns between capital and labour, 1 per cent of the UK GDP in 2004 would be £9 billion. This is the amount workers lose to capital. Approximately 50 per cent of capital's returns are used for capital formation, so, following Borjas, one could generally estimate the increased capital formation due to the immigrant-induced fall in native labour wages to be about £5 billion.

The target required for immigrant wealth to match native wealth is 10 per cent of the total national wealth (remember, immigrants are taking care of the £2,235 annual increase required out of their wages and enterprise profits, unless they are making foreign remittances), which is £424 billion; at £5 billion per annum, this would take 85 years to reach – 85 years to achieve equality with natives.

However, there are three further problems.

The first is a simple interest effect. Someone has to be paid for supplying immigrants with wealth while they have not got any. For example, if it is imported, there will be a drain of interest. The other alternative is for wealth to be appropriated from natives. It is clear that the interest effects on £424 billion alone would swamp the £5 billion capital formation.

The second problem is that, as Borjas points out, the immigrant surplus, which causes distribution from native wages to capital, shrinks as immigrants and their children take up native skills – in his example, the skills of US workers.

Third, as the immigrants become better equipped with capital (at £5 billion per annum) this also shrinks the immigration surplus and the extra returns to capital caused by immigration. As Borjas says, 'the immigration surplus will tend to become smaller and smaller'.

Borjas himself does not do the calculations, but he appears to suggest that the difference in skills shrinks by 50 per cent in one generation, and a further 25 per cent in the second generation. This would mean the benefits to capital formation would shrink to £2.5 billion per annum after 30 years and to £1.25 billion per annum after 60 years. After 85 years, the capital generated would be not £424 billion, but somewhere in the region of £250 billion.

He makes no calculation for the shrinkage in returns to capital as the capital stock grows. This would reduce the £250 billion further and, if we assume the same shrinkage rate as applied to the shrinkage in the skills' differential, this would imply the extra capital would reduce to about £150 billion, assuming there were no foreign remittances – a long way below the £424 billion required to avoid dilution of the wealth of natives.

A great deal more analysis needs to be done on the statistics of capital adjustment on all three problems mentioned above.

These figures are very rough and may be regarded as speculative. It should be remembered that, throughout the process, wages of native workers are reduced so as to produce higher returns to capital, which, in turn, supplies the capital formation required by immigrants.

Simultaneously, there will be a fall in savings by native workers, and this should be deducted from the amounts available to generate capital adjustment. This has not been calculated.

The British government

It is now worth briefly turning to the argument put forward by those who say that immigration has no depressing effects on native wages.

Then Prime Minister Tony Blair said in his speech to the TUC in 2006: 'If migrant workers are treated fairly and paid a decent wage, they represent no threat to the livelihood of people who are already living and working in the UK.'

Of course, if we take Mr Blair's view that immigration has no depressing effect on native wages, then, as Borjas indicates, we are in for a shock:

> … there is no immigration surplus, if the native wage is not reduced by immigration.
>
> In other words, if some workers are not harmed by immigration, many of the benefits that are typically attributed to immigration – higher profits for firms, lower prices for consumers – cease to exist. As I pointed out earlier, no pain, no gain.[31]

The pro-immigration argument based on the 'immigration surplus' – a GDP effect that ignores wealth and capital, and that is anyway very small – is completely irrelevant if native wages are not reduced.

One can extend this argument further because of its implications for wealth. If the Mr Blair is right, and there is no fall in wages for native workers, then there is no 85-year-long march to the £424 billion or £250 billion of capital (or £150 billion) that is required to equip immigrants with the same wealth as natives and that free market economists think may be supplied by the extra returns to capital following immigration-induced falls in native wages. There is no extra return for capitalists and no capital adjustment. The whole argument for immigration disintegrates. The British people will find themselves financing immigrants' stake capital of £141,000 per worker, and this can only be achieved by depressing the wealth of British natives. Indeed, there is simply massive crowding-in on the existing capital of natives, with no capital being provided by immigrants, except for their £2,235 annual contribution (or £988 allowing for foreign remittances; which, of course, means that the average immigrant's annual contribution to capital additions must be topped back up to £2,235 by appropriation from natives).

Conclusion

Whether you believe Mr Blair or the careful studies of US economists, in a free economy it is unlikely that immigration will ever pay for the wealth required to put immigrants on a par with natives – unless the immigrants bring skills and capital that are superior to those of the natives. Failing this, there must inevitably be wealth dilution for the natives.

The native workers in the USA and Britain have come to the correct conclusion. Immigration decreases their wages and their wealth. The major parties and the political classes have it wrong.

Free market economists who advocate the free movement of labour must include the effects of migration on wealth in their calculations.

Appendix A –

The Immigration Surplus

(reproduced from *The New Americans*, p. 139)

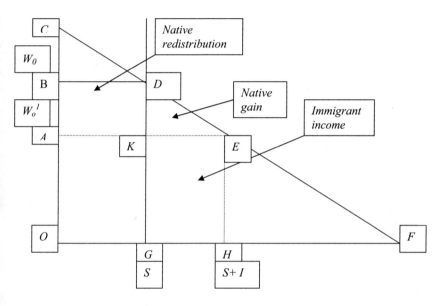

Figure 4.1: The immigration surplus

In the simple world portrayed by this diagram, we have two types of domestic workers: those that are perfect substitutes for immigrants (unskilled labour) and those that are complements (skilled labour).[†] Only one good is produced (GDP), and the numbers of unskilled and skilled domestic workers are fixed. Figure 4.1 plots the demand curve (*CF*) for domestic unskilled workers.

Before immigration, there are S domestic, unskilled workers, who are all paid a wage W_0 (the wage that equates demand and supply), so that the total amount that domestic unskilled workers are paid is S times W_0 or the area *OBDG*. Although we deal explicitly only with unskilled workers in this diagram, we can also determine how much skilled domestic workers are paid. To see this, note that the height at each point along the demand curve is the value of the extra national output produced by another unskilled worker. Therefore, total national output (GDP) is the area below the demand curve up to S unskilled workers

---

[†] In particular in this simple world, there is no capital, so that workers receive all the income produced by selling the single good.

(*OCDG*), so that the remainder (*BCD*) is the amount paid to domestic skilled workers.

Now, let new immigrants come into this country, increasing the supply of all unskilled labour in the workforce to *S+I*. The new wage that equates the demand and supply of unskilled labour falls to W_0^1; that is, the wage of substitute domestic unskilled workers falls to W_0^1. Unskilled domestic workers are clearly worse off. Since the total amount that all unskilled domestic workers are paid falls to *OAKG*, the domestic unskilled workers lose *ABDK* as a result of immigration. Unskilled immigrants are paid the same wage as domestic unskilled workers so, as a group, immigrants receive the area *GKEH*.

What about skilled domestic workers? Before immigration, they received the area *BCD*, but what do they get now? Once again, we can calculate their incomes as a residual. With these new immigrants added to the workforce, total national output (GDP) will rise, so that it now equals the area under the demand curve up to the total number of unskilled workers, *S+I*. Instead of their pre-immigration incomes of *BCD*, domestic skilled labour now receives the area *ACE* (everything that isn't paid to either unskilled domestic workers or immigrants). Total GDP is now the area *OCEH*, so that the value of domestic output has increased by the area *GDEH*. But new immigrants get only the rectangle *GKEH*, so that, on net, domestic workers must gain by the size of the triangle *KDE*. Immigration thus raises national output and national output per domestic worker.

One way of seeing that the native born must gain from immigration in this simple model is to recognize that new immigrants help produce new goods and services, but they are paid less than the total value of these new goods and services. The rest goes to domestic residents, who collectively are better off than before, by the triangle *KDE*.

Figure 4.1 also illustrates that, although the net gain is positive domestically, some workers may lose and others may gain. In fact, although domestic unskilled workers lose *ABDK*, domestic skilled workers gain *ABDE*. The area in common is the rectangle *ABDK*, which is simultaneously (and equally) a loss to unskilled domestic workers and a gain to skilled domestic workers.

Therefore, although immigration yields a positive net gain to domestic workers, that gain is not spread equally: it harms workers who are substitutes for immigrants, and benefits workers who are complements to immigrants. Most economists believe that unskilled domestic workers are the substitutes, so their wages will fall, and skilled domestic workers are complements, so their wages will rise.

Appendix B

What should a migrant earn in the UK in 2007 to make a contribution to the economy?

Migration Watch calculates (Briefing Paper No. 1.11) that the required income 'to make a positive contribution to GDP per capita' is about £27,000 p.a. (2006). Migration Watch is to be congratulated on making an estimate, and this study has followed its methodology in part.

The Migration Watch estimate is calculated in three parts:

1. The amount of UK GDP classified by National Statistics as 'compensation for employees' in the year 2003 was £613 billion and there were 27.6 million workers. This gives average earnings per worker of £22,200. There is also earned income included in the category 'mixed income', but this is ignored for these rough calculations.

2. This is then increased to 2006 rates by allowing three years of wage inflation at 4 per cent per year, making roughly £24,850 p.a.

3. Migration Watch then allows a 10 per cent margin requirement for the costs of additional infrastructure at £2,485 p.a., making £27,335. (Migration Watch rounds this to £27,000 p.a.)

All the income calculations seem reasonable, but a 10 per cent margin for the costs of additional infrastructure is not realistic and there seems to be no basis for using this figure. (In these calculations I have ignored the supposed benefits of capital adjustment, because this implies a fall in the wages of native workers.)

This study shows that a worker requires instant wealth of £141,000 on arrival (2004 figures), so the question is to determine how many years should be allowed to pay this off and, second, the rate of interest that should be imposed.

For this exercise, we have taken an interest rate of 3 per cent and spread the cost of financing the instant wealth over a working life of, say, 35 years. These are, of course, assumptions only.

In order to do the calculation, we must first bring our wealth figure for 2004 up to date for the end of 2006. (It will be noted that this figure was originally at 2003 prices in the National Statistics tables.) So, three years of inflation need to be added to bring the £141,000 up to 2006 prices. This can be estimated at 9 per cent, making the figure £153,600. There have also been two further years of capital additions, which, we will assume, were at the 2004 rate of 1.58 per cent of wealth. These additions add a further, say, 3 per cent, or £4,500, making total wealth per head at the end of 2006 around £158,000 in 2006 prices. We thus now have the total wealth at the end of 2006 in 2006 prices per worker.

Compound interest tables inform us that, to pay off £158,000 with an interest rate of 3 per cent over 35 years, there must be a yearly payment of capital and interest of £7,300. So, instead of the £2,485 p.a. estimated by Migration Watch, the real figure to be added to average earnings is £7,300. The income required to be earned by a migrant is, therefore, £22,200 (the average earnings in 2003) plus 12 per cent wage inflation of, say, £2,650 – which totals £24,850 – plus £7,300: this equals £32,150. Looking at Inland Revenue taxation figures for 2004/5, the latest year available, 5,769,000 out of the 27,020,000 taxpayers who paid tax on earned income from employment and self-employment earned over £30,000 per annum (or 21.35 per cent of taxpayers paying tax on earned income).[‡]

So the calculation is that an immigrant who makes no foreign remittances would have to be in the top 20 per cent of earners, with taxable earnings in 2006 of £32,150, for him to contribute to increasing the average per capita GDP of natives.

Should foreign remittances be made, these would have to be added to the above figure. We saw earlier that, in 2003, £3.8 billion was remitted abroad. This means the average remittance per immigrant worker is £1,247 p.a.; £32,150 plus £1,247 makes a grand total of £33,397.

When considering family migration, a family of four requires £282,000 (in 2004) of instant wealth in the original calculation. The answer to the question of what the income of an immigrant family of four should be, taking the above, up-to-date calculations: it should be £33,397 x 2 = £66,794, i.e. double what an individual worker requires.

These calculations leave out any fiscal costs, transitional costs and long-term national identity costs.

[‡] Source: Table 3.6 of Income Tax & Personal Incomes, Inland Revenue Statistics for 2004/5.

Notes and references

[1] Migration Watch UK, 'Economic contribution of A8 migrants', Briefing Paper 1.12, available at www.migrationwatchuk.org/pdfs/economic/1_12_Economic_contribution_of_A8migrants.pdf

[2] *The Ground of Justice – Draft Report of a Pastoral Research Enquiry into the Needs of Migrants in London's Catholic Community*, Centre for the Study of Faith in Society, Von Hügel Institute, St Edmund's College, University of Cambridge, available at www.st-edmunds.cam.ac.uk/vhi/index.shtml

[3] Available at www.worldviews.org/detailreports/usreport.pdf p. 42.

[4] Speaking at a press conference hosted by the Center for Immigration Studies, Washington, 17 December 2002.

[5] Speaking at the same press conference by the Center for Immigration Studies.

[6] Anthony Scholefield, 'Britain's demographic profile is changing at a bewildering rate', *Eurofacts*, 15 December 2006, available at www.junepress.com/PDF/Vol%2012%20No%20%205%20and%206%20-%2015th%20December%202006.pdf

[7] Sir Digby Jones in the *Sunday Telegraph*, 20 August 2006.

[8] *New Statesman*, 11 September 2006.

[9] George J. Borjas, *Heaven's Door*, Princeton, NJ: Princeton University Press, 1999, p. 212.

[10] National Research Council of the National Academy of Science, Commission on Behavioral and Social Sciences and Education (CBASSE), *The New Americans: Economic, Demographic and Fiscal Effects of Immigration*, Washington, DC: National Academies Press, 1997, p. 146.

[11] *Ibid.*, p. 146.

[12] *Ibid.*, p. 137.

[13] *Ibid.*, p. 141.

[14] *Ibid.*, p. 141.

[15] *Ibid.*, p. 158.

[16] Luke Johnson in the *Sunday Telegraph*, 17 September 2006.

[17] NRC, *The Immigration Debate; Studies on the Economic, Demographic and Fiscal Effects of Immigration*, eds. James P. Smith and Barry Edmonston, Washington, DC: National Academies Press, 1998, p. 315.

[18] Borjas, *Heaven's Door*, p. 88.

[19] NRC, *The New Americans*, p. 147.

[20] Borjas, *Heaven's Door*, p. 87.

[21] *The New Americans*, p.158.

[22] *Ibid.*, p. 158.

[23] Henry Hazlitt, *Economics in One Lesson*, San Francisco: Laissez Faire Books, 1996.

[24] National Statistics, *Capital Stocks, Capital Consumption and Non-Financial Balance Sheets*, 2005. All statistics from this publication. See in particular tables 2.1.1 and following. Available at http://www.statistics.gov.uk/downloads/theme_economy/capitalstocks2005.pdf

[25] CPB Netherlands Bureau for Economic Policy Analysis, 'Immigration and the Dutch economy', table 3.2, available at www.cpb.nl/eng/pub/cpbreeksen/bijzonder/47/bijz47.pdf

[26] John Meadowcroft in the *Journal of the Institute of Economic Affairs*, March 2006.

[27] NRC, *The Immigration Debate,* p. 333.

[28] *Ibid.*, p. 319.

[29] *Ibid.*, p. 320.

[30] Borjas, *Heaven's Door*, p. 96.

[31] *Ibid.*, p. 96.